# VICTORIA WOODHULL
## *First Woman Presidential Candidate*

Notable Americans

# VICTORIA WOODHULL
## *First Woman Presidential Candidate*

**Jacqueline McLean**

MORGAN
REYNOLDS
Incorporated

Greensboro

**VICTORIA WOODHULL** *First Woman Presidential Candidate*

Photo credits: Library of Congress; New York Public Library; New York Historical
Society.

Library of Congress Cataloging-in-Publication Data
McLean, Jacqueline.
    Victoria Woodhull : first presidential candidate / Jacqueline McLean.—1st ed.
      p. cm. — (Notable Americans)
    Includes bibliographical references (p. ) and index.
    Summary: Examines the life of nineteenth century feminist, Victoria Woodhull,
who was a selected as the presidential candidate for the Equal Rights Party in 1872.
    ISBN 1-883846-47-1 (lib. bdg.)
    1. Woodhull, Victoria C. (Victoria Claflin), 1838-1927—Juvenile literature.
2. Women—United States—Biography—Juvenile literature. 3. Women in politics—
United States—Biography—Juvenile literature. 4. Feminists—United States—
Biography—Juvenile literature. 5. Electioneering—United States—History—Juvenile
literature. 6. Presidential candidates—United States—Juvenile literature. [1. Woodhull,
Victoria C. (Victoria Claflin), 1838-1927 . 2. Feminists. 3. Presidential candidates.
4. Women—Biography.]
    I. Title. II. Series.

HQ1413.W66 M37 1999
305.42'092—dc21
[B]

99-032946

Printed in the United States of America

First Edition

*For Alex*

# CONTENTS

*Victoria Woodhull*

# Chapter One

---

## A Turbulent Childhood

Annie Claflin was a superstitious woman. She believed that a dog howling near a window was a sure sign of coming death, as was a fruit tree that blossomed in the autumn. When Annie gave birth to a daughter on September 23, 1838, she named the child "Victoria" after the eighteen-year-old queen of England. It was a funny name for a girl who would eventually grow up to fight against the lot of women in the Victorian era. The Victorians believed a woman's place was in the home. Her role in life was to care for her husband and her children, to be the family's moral center—the "Angel in the House."

When Annie Claflin chose the name "Victoria" for her daughter, she wasn't thinking about women's rights or social decorum. "Victoria" was simply a beautiful name with a regal ring to it. It was a name for Annie to build her hopes upon. The Claflins were poor and lacked formal education and Annie hoped that with such a name her daughter would be victorious in whatever she attempted.

The fifth of seven living children, Victoria grew up in a twenty-five-foot-long frame house on the outskirts of the small town of Homer, Ohio. Though the little girl had been named for a queen, the beginnings of Victoria's own life were far from luxurious. There was very little privacy in the Claflin household, and with so many children, everyone in the family was expected to help out.

From early childhood onwards, young Victoria was given a great deal of responsibility. She spent many afternoons helping her mother to bake bread and make such household items as candles and soap. In the summer, the vegetable garden needed spading and watering, and during autumn and winter, firewood had to be brought in from out-of-doors. By the age of five Victoria was looking after her younger sisters, Utica and Tennessee. When Tennessee was sick with a fever, it was Victoria who stayed up late rocking her baby sister's cradle and singing lullabies to ease the baby's sleep.

Victoria had two imaginary friends who talked and played with her as she did her chores. She named them Delia and Odessa Maldiva after two of her sisters who had died before she was born. One night, walking with her mother to a nightly prayer meeting at the Methodist Church, Victoria suddenly grabbed her mother and begged her to stop and listen to the voices on the air. The voices told her that two men were getting ready to rob the Claflin home. She convinced her mother to return to the house and light a lamp in each room to frighten the robbers away.

Victoria's mother, Annie Claflin, could recite long Bible passages from memory.

It was hard for an imaginative and intelligent girl like Victoria to always concentrate on her adult-sized responsibilities. She sometimes wandered off when she was supposed to be collecting firewood, or ate many of the vegetables she picked in the garden. Victoria found caring for Tennessee especially difficult. Sometimes she fell asleep on the job. Once while watching her sister, Victoria awoke to the sound of footsteps and realized with a stab of fear that her mother had caught her sleeping. Afraid of a scolding, Victoria quickly came up with an imaginative explanation. She told her mother that she hadn't been sleeping at all. It was something greater and more mysterious. She'd had a vision. "The angels put me in a trance," Victoria explained. "That's why my eyes were closed."

At first, her mother was skeptical of her daughter's explanation, but when Victoria went on to describe in detail the two angels who had come to look after Tennessee, Annie became more interested. Victoria spoke excitedly of the way the angels had guided her hands away from the cradle so that they could care for the feverish baby on their own. In the end, Annie Claflin became convinced that her five-year-old daughter was telling the truth. After all, it was Annie who first predicted that her Victoria would be an exceptional child.

As she grew older, Victoria became more prone to religious visions. This is not surprising. Annie Claflin was a deeply religious person, and though Annie could not read, she was able to recite long Bible passages from memory. Victoria learned to pattern herself after her mother. They attended religious revival meetings together. On Sundays Victoria accompanied her mother to services at the Methodist Church. As the candles flickered on the altar, Victoria watched her mother go into religious ecstasies, calling out "Hallelujah!" Though others considered Annie to be eccentric, Victoria accepted her mother's behavior. A passionate response seemed appropriate to Victoria, especially when God and salvation were concerned. For a poor girl whose family was not accepted by the community, the possibility of religious salvation held tremendous power.

During this formative period in her life, Victoria became convinced that God had put her on the earth to do more than the average person. In one of her visions a young man in a tunic told her that she was destined for great things. "One day, you will lead your people," the young man said. In later years, looking back on her own beginnings, Victoria wrote, "I know that my companions from the moment of birth were heaven's choicest souls. I grew side by side with them, in fact all the education and inspiration came [through] them."

While Victoria's mother was a faithful churchgoer who instilled in her daughter a respect for religion, Victoria's father, Buck Claflin, was something else altogether. An adventurer, and by some accounts a real rascal, Buck was always on the lookout for a chance to make some fast money. He held more than a dozen jobs, but was not particularly successful at any of them. He spent his early years as a horse dealer and trainer. He enjoyed this work because it offered plenty of opportunities for spirited conversations and cold ale at the local taverns.

Buck hung out with gamblers and horse traders until he landed a job cutting and hauling lumber along the Susquehanna River. It was in one of these river towns that he met and married Annie Hummel, the daughter of a local tavern owner. In the coming months, Buck's work on the construction of the Ohio and Erie canals brought his wife and children to Homer a few years before Victoria's birth.

Homer, Ohio was a conservative small town in the middle of the state. Surrounded by farms and endless stretches of open country, Homer was a tidy spot with well-kept streets in the middle of a vast rural landscape. There were few public buildings: a log cabin school, a post office, a general store, a church, and the grain mill that was owned by Buck Claflin. Only 300 people lived in Homer, and most were nothing like the Claflins, who were neither accepted nor liked by their neighbors. People were suspicious of Annie's strange religious zeal, and they didn't trust Buck.

Victoria grew to be a confident child in spite of these disadvantages. Standing atop the Williams Farm Indian Mound (which she renamed the Mount of Olives), she recited Bible stories to the children gathered around her. "Sinners, repent!" she'd cry out before beginning a tale, mimicking the words used to open a revival meeting. When her audience became restless Victoria abandoned religion for tales of adventure.

At school in Homer, Victoria's intelligence soon became obvious. She had a photographic memory and could look at a page of text and then repeat it back by heart. Because she was a girl, however, neither her parents nor her teachers placed great emphasis on her education. It would be several years before the state instituted any formal rules about education. While Victoria was growing up, children of all ages gathered together in a one-room schoolhouse when there was a teacher available for instruction. Regular classroom hours came only later, as did the separation of children by grade.

Victoria only attended school from ages eight to eleven. Nevertheless, she displayed a passion for learning. She earned the nickname of "the little queen" because of her proud demeanor and her intense power of concentration. Very early on in life she came to understand that knowledge could lead to better things. She may have been poor, but Victoria was already proving her fierce determination to succeed. She wanted a better life. She just wasn't sure—yet—how to get it.

Life in Homer may not have been easy for the Claflins, but it was the only home Victoria had ever known. Though Buck Claflin was sometimes out of work, the family was generally able to make ends meet. A loud and boisterous crew, they often fought amongst themselves. Buck was an especially harsh disciplinarian. But they were fiercely loyal to each other and always defended one another against outsiders. The Claflins' loyalty and solidarity helped make a hard life bearable, and on the whole, they were relatively happy—until the winter of 1853.

Buck Claflin owned the town's grain mill. Grinding the neighboring farmers' wheat and oats provided the family a basic living. Then, on a bitterly cold night, the mill caught fire when a burning lamp overturned. Though the townspeople organized themselves to put out the flames, in less than an hour nothing was left but a few charred beams. Worse yet, on the night of the fire Buck was away from home, leaving Annie and her children to face the catastrophe on their own. Victoria never forgot the frigid night she stood shivering on a nearby bridge with the others and watched as the mill—and any chance of financial prosperity for the family—vanished.

Though the townspeople worked together to put out the fire, after the catastrophe no one rallied around the Claflins. A number of people accused Buck of setting fire to the mill himself in order to collect the insurance money. No one ever established if the accusation was true, and Buck was never formally charged with arson, but the rumor persisted. Life became so difficult for the Claflins that they decided it was time to leave Homer, Ohio. They

Many citizens of Homer, Ohio did not trust Victoria's father, Buck Claflin.

packed up their belongings and headed for the nearby town of Mount Gilead, where Victoria's eldest sister, Maggie, and her family lived.

In Mount Gilead, the Claflins moved into the American House, a hotel owned by Maggie's husband, Enos Miles. From this time onwards fourteen-year-old Victoria and her youngest sister, Tennessee, who was just eleven, became the family's main financial support.

How did these two girls support a family that included Annie and Buck as well as their sixteen-year-old brother, Maldon, and thirteen-year-old Utica? Victoria and Tennessee (or "Tennie" as she was fondly called), became spiritual mediums, and they were paid well for the work. The mid-1800s proved to be a time of intense interest in "clairvoyance," the term for this occult form of communication with the beyond. Two occurrences increased America's interest in this otherworldly form of communication.

The invention of the telegraph in 1848 proved that the human voice could travel from one point to another in a mysterious fashion. At the time, most people didn't understand the principles of telegraphy (and its connection to electricity), well enough to distinguish between the instantaneous communication of messages over long distances by wires, and the communication of messages between this world and the next through a human medium. In fact, people began to refer to clairvoyance as a form of spiritual telegraphy. Ultimately, for much of the general public, the workings of the telegraph was proof enough of extrasensory forces at work in the universe. This opened their minds to the possibility of supernatural encounters.

In addition to the invention of the telegraph, the religious revival of the first half of the century, known as the Second Great Awakening, fostered a belief that any person—and not just a priest or a minister—could speak directly to God. Some people came to believe in the possibility of communicating with those beyond the grave. After all, if an ordinary person could talk to God, then what was there to stop a person from reaching a lost loved one?

Though women in the nineteenth century were generally discouraged from speaking in public, they could speak publicly in a religious context. During the Second Great Awakening, the number of female religious leaders increased. Women also became important figures in the growing popularity of spiritual telepathy. Spiritual mediums were the "vehicles" through which other voices spoke. If a woman acted as a medium, she was not held responsible for what the voices speaking through her said. As a result, the role of spiritual medium offered many women the opportunity to have a good deal of influence in their communities. It also provided them an opportunity to make money.

In the beginning it was Buck Claflin who pushed his daughters in spiritualism. He was not interested in their talents—he hoped that they would make the family rich. Buck had heard of two famous mediums, a pair of New York sisters by the names of Kate and Margaret Fox, who were earning a phenomenal amount of money from their seances.

In the beginning, Victoria and Tennessee were not aware of the controversy surrounding their strange new profession, or the opportunities it presented to them. Though Victoria had always felt that she was special, she was uncertain how to go about her new work as a spiritual medium. After her father had hung a sign outside their door to advertize the girls as clairvoyants, Victoria asked what she should do. Buck had only one piece of advice: "Be a good listener, child."

# Chapter Two

## Marriage

During the autumn of 1853, when she was fifteen, Victoria met Doctor Canning Woodhull, the man who became her first husband and whose surname she was to keep for the rest of her life. At the time of their meeting, Canning Woodhull was a striking man of twenty-eight with dark hair and eyes and an appealing manner. The Claflins first called Dr. Woodhull to treat Victoria's rheumatism and fever. Upon meeting his young patient, the doctor quickly found himself captivated by her beauty and intelligence. When Victoria recovered, he decided to court her, and after only one date Canning proposed marriage. Victoria later remembered him saying, "Tell your father and mother that I want you for a wife."

The Claflins were impressed by Canning Woodhull's credentials. He claimed that his father was a famous judge and that his uncle was the mayor of New York City. Though Victoria was not as taken with Canning as her parents were, she was pleased to have such a handsome suitor. She was attracted to the storybook marriages that she had read about in books and magazines. As one of seven children in a poor family, marriage seemed an especially bright way to escape her past hardships. As a married woman, Victoria believed that she'd have her own house with a husband who adored her. With this notion in the forefront of her mind, on November 23, 1853, Victoria married the doctor and became Victoria Claflin Woodhull.

Though Doctor Canning Woodhull made a strong first impression, the young bride soon became disillusioned with her new husband when she discovered that he had built his reputation on a string of lies. Though he claimed that his father was a prominent judge, in reality, he was a justice of the peace. As for being related to the mayor of New York, there was a former mayor named Caleb Woodhull, but he bore no relation to Victoria's husband. Worse yet, though Canning told Victoria that he was a successful doctor, in reality, he had very few patients. He and Victoria had to move from place to place to find work.

Victoria was used to living in difficult financial circumstances. Because of her own unsettled childhood she could have borne these hardships. What she could not bear was her new husband's alcoholism. Canning Woodhull often stayed out all night squandering the little money he earned on drink. Sometimes he even spent the night with other women. Looking back on these terrible discoveries about her new husband Victoria said, "In a single day, I grew ten years older. The shock awoke all my womanhood."

In spite of these difficulties, Victoria managed to survive the first year of marriage, and gradually she learned to live with her alcoholic husband. After all, she had no other choice. Under the law a married woman, her wealth, and her future children all belonged to her husband. In other words, Victoria Claflin Woodhull was trapped.

Though she hated housekeeping, there was no one else to do the work, so Victoria did the best she could. Often the bread went unbaked and the clothes unmended. Canning was usually too drunk to notice.

Life continued in this haphazard fashion for a while. In December of 1854 the Woodhulls were living in Chicago when Victoria gave birth to her first child, a boy, whom the couple named Byron. In the beginning, Victoria was thrilled with her beautiful child, and she began to build big plans around Byron's future. These plans crumbled when Victoria learned that Byron was mentally retarded. This was a great shock that also made the couple feel guilty. In the mid-nineteenth century most people did not understand the causes of mental retardation. It was often attributed to some sin or failing on the part of the parents. Victoria became convinced that her son's condition had been caused by his father's alcoholism.

Although learning of Byron's condition was a terrible shock, Victoria had no intentions of giving up. The Claflins had always moved when they found themselves in trouble, and Victoria was no different from the rest of her family in this respect. In 1855, when Byron was still a baby, sixteen-year-old Victoria moved her small family west to San Francisco, hoping to find a better life. Though the gold rush was over by the time the Woodhulls arrived, San Francisco was one of the fastest growing cities in America, and Victoria had youth and the ambition it took to succeed.

Her first job in San Francisco was as a dressmaker, one of the few respectable jobs available to women. One of Victoria's clients was Anna Cogswell, a popular actress who headed up her own theater company. Anna saw something special in Victoria and asked her to join her acting company. Victoria began with small parts and eventually, as her confidence and diction improved, she moved into leading parts. Soon she was earning fifty-two dollars a week, a comfortable sum. Victoria's stage work also helped her develop poise, elegant manners, and a lovely speaking voice.

Victoria did not want to spend her life in the theater, however. "I do not care for the stage," she said, "and I shall leave it at the first opportunity."

This opportunity came in a typically unusual way. One night, while performing in a play called *The Corsican Brothers*, a spirit voice came to her on-stage and said, "Victoria, come home." As she stood there in the middle of a scene, Victoria became convinced that it was Tennessee's image she saw in the distance beckoning to her. Not even bothering to finish the performance, Victoria left the theater and raced home through the fog to her hotel. She packed up the family's things and first thing

Victoria had a vision of her sister Tennessee beckoning her to return to Ohio.

the next morning the three Woodhulls were on board a steamer bound for New York. After landing in New York, they rode trains to the Claflin home in Ohio where Victoria found Tennessee dressed in the same calico jumper she'd seen in the vision. When Victoria asked her mother for an explanation about what had happened, Annie Claflin confessed that a few weeks earlier she had told Tennessee, "My dear, send the spirits after Victoria to bring her home."

The Claflins soon discovered that the daughter who returned to Ohio was a changed person from the newly married girl who had left a few years before. Victoria had grown up fast. She was a serious and hardworking woman with a tough view of how the world worked and of male-female relationships.

Fourteen-year-old Tennessee was now the Claflin's major breadwinner. Tennessee was earning up to one hundred dollars a day as a spiritual medium. Victoria soon returned to working as a medium, also.

Victoria earned more than money from her work as a medium. She took her role very seriously and found both self-respect and emotional satisfaction in this career. She stitched the words of Psalm 120 into her sleeve to keep herself honest: "Deliver my soul O Lord from lying lips and from a deceitful tongue."

Victoria used no medicines in her practice. She relied solely on the power of her touch and her abilities as a listener. With her lovely voice and penetrating dark eyes, Victoria was a reassuring presence, and her clients quickly

Victoria with husband, Canning Woodhull, and their children, Byron and Zula.

opened up to her. In this era before psychoanalysis and psychology, mediums (as well as ministers and priests) served as counselors for people who had few places to turn.

Even if Victoria did not have all the powers she claimed, she did possess compassion and considerable life experience, both of which helped her assist the people who came to her. Like many of her female patients, Victoria knew what it was like to live with a husband who was often drunk and unable to provide for his family. As the child of the Claflins, she understood how it felt to be an outcast.

All this life experience served Victoria well in her occupation. Women abused by their husbands told her of violent marriages. Forlorn men came to her as well to confess their unhappiness in marriage and to seek her advice. Her work as a medium helped to form her belief that divorce was often necessary to assure an individual's happiness. These experiences were preparing her for her later role as a fiercely determined women's and human rights advocate.

During the late 1850s, Victoria moved often in order to find work. Sometimes she traveled with her extended family, other times with Canning and her son. She crossed such states as Indiana, Illinois, Pennsylvania, Arkansas, and Missouri. In all these places, she lived and worked as a medium in either a hotel or a rented house.

On April 23, 1861 Victoria gave birth to a daughter whom she named Zulu or Zula Maud. No one knows for certain why Victoria chose the unusual name of "Zulu," the name of an African tribe as well as a nineteenth century name for a dark tulip that may have been in bloom at the time of the birth. The birth of a healthy baby girl was a godsend for Victoria because it freed her at last from the guilt and anguish she suffered over Byron.

In the months that followed Zula Maud's birth, life changed drastically for America. The Civil War broke out in April of 1861 over the explosive issue of slavery, which had long divided the nation. The United States was plunged into crisis. The Land of Liberty became a broken country: a landscape of disease and destruction. Three million men went to war, and nearly seven hundred thousand died in the four years of fighting. Many soldiers died of diseases like typhoid, malaria, and pneumonia.

During the war, Victoria continued to travel and work as a spiritual medium. People were hungry for answers during these terrible years and many turned to clairvoyance. There was little fighting in the mid-west, so she and her family stuck to this part of the country.

In 1864, Victoria and Tennessee settled in St. Louis, where Victoria met Colonel James Harvey Blood, the man who became her second husband. A native of Massachusetts who had relocated to St. Louis, Blood was just back from the Civil War. Tall and broad-shouldered with dark good looks and a commanding presence, Victoria found herself immediately taken with him.

Blood was one of the founders of the St. Louis Society of Spiritualists, and at the time of his meeting with

Victoria he was serving as its president. Yet it was as a patient and not a colleague that Blood came to see Victoria in the offices she shared with Tennessee. What he came to consult Victoria about remains unclear. What is clear, however, is that their first meeting had a monumental impact on both of them. Victoria supposedly passed into a trance! Seated opposite the impressive Civil War veteran, in a faraway-sounding voice Victoria told Blood that "his future destiny was to be linked with hers in marriage." The Colonel was not shocked by Victoria's announcement. When Victoria recovered from her trance she and the Colonel became engaged—in spite of the fact that both were still legally married.

Because they were both spiritualists, the couple believed that the spiritual affinity they felt in each other's company was much more powerful than the marriage bonds that bound them to other people. Therefore, despite the social stigma attached to the dissolution of marriage at the time, the pair swiftly filed for divorce. They were eventually married on July 12, 1866 in Dayton, Ohio.

After the wedding, they relocated to Pittsburgh, Pennsylvania. Victoria's two children accompanied them. Victoria did not give up Canning Woodhull's name, which she considered to be rightfully her own. Besides, it was the name belonging to both her children. Because of Victoria's choice, however, people often believed that she and James Blood were not legally married. Victoria did not care.

At their first meeting Victoria told Colonel James Blood that "his future destiny was to be linked to hers in marriage."

Although she was attached to her first husband's last name, Victoria adored James Blood's strength and commitment. His dynamism and ambition spurred Victoria on and made her feel much more secure. At the age of twenty-six, Victoria began to thrive. In many ways, Victoria's second husband became her first real mentor, exposing her to the radical new ideas of their time such as birth control, free education, and equal rights for women.

Victoria had endured many hardships in her first marriage and had witnessed and treated much suffering in her travels across the United States. These experiences made her eager to embrace the new thinking that seemed to offer greater individual liberty and freedom to a highly intelligent woman like herself. She saw no reason why she or other gifted people should be held back by society's rules and strictures. Clearly these rules were in place to keep one group of people in a more powerful position than others. She believed in a society based on talent and ability—not sex and class.

Colonel Blood helped Victoria solidify her thinking on these issues. The colonel's ideas made her remember her early years in the Methodist Church in Homer, Ohio. She saw a clear connection between these new ideas and the minister's sermons about finding a better life on this earth through the idealistic teachings of Christianity. Soon, Victoria was as passionate about and as committed to social reform as was her new husband.

# Chapter Three

## New York City

In 1868, while Victoria and Colonel Blood were living in Pittsburgh, Victoria had a vision that she later described:

> One night...[my principal spirit guide] suddenly appeared and began to write upon the table. The letters were of fire and lighted up the room distinctly. When done he turned and commanded me to read. I did so, and it was, 'Depart thence'....I was to go to New York....There, in New York, I would find the house I was to occupy at number 17 Great Jones Street, which had been prepared for me.

We do not know if Victoria's vision actually happened. It is true that Victoria and her extended family did make a home at 17 Great Jones Street in New York City.

In the years following war, New York City, along with the rest of the United States, grew rapidly. This was an era of rapid industrialization and as factories sprung up throughout the once empty countryside many fortunes were made—and lost—in the process. After their arrival, Victoria and her extended family soon realized that New York was a more suitable place for them to live and work than the mid-west. New York was made up of contradictions and extremes, and the eccentricities of the Claflins and Colonel Blood did not attract so much negative attention. The city bustled with gamblers, tattoo artists, beggars, as well as businessmen and ordinary folk, and was the home of the wealthiest people in America as well as the country's poorest immigrants.

Life in New York stimulated Victoria and gave her a wider arena for her talents and energy. She was able to expand her growing interest in women's rights. Victoria knew now that to become a player in the fight for equality she needed money. Most of the well-known women's rights activists came from the upper and upper-middle class. Their financial security gave them freedom and power not enjoyed by poorer women.

Victoria and Tennessee set themselves up as spiritual mediums. But this profession was not as lucrative as before. After the Civil War the government instituted new medical standards that prevented spiritualists from claiming medical expertise. During the Civil War her father had induced Tennessee to claim the ability to cure cancer. This claim resulted in disaster when one of her patients died and Tennessee was charged with manslaughter.

Never again did either sister claim medical expertise. Their New York business cards simply read: "Mrs. Victoria Woodhull and Miss Tennie C. Claflin, clairvoyants."

One of the sisters' first clients was the seventy-three-year-old multi-millionaire, Commodore Cornelius Vanderbilt, whom they approached at his home on a mild spring day in 1868. Though the Commodore had made a fortune in railroads and shipping, he was a no-nonsense man with few social airs. The Commodore was also susceptible to female beauty and charm and Tennessee and Victoria were an irresistible combination. Soon the Commodore was seeking out the sisters for advice on a number of matters. "Do as I do, consult the spirits," became one of the Commodore's favorite expressions.

The Commodore genuinely liked Victoria and Tennessee (he may have become Tennessee's lover), but it is hard to determine how much he actually relied upon their spiritual powers in making his business deals. He did take both women under his wing and taught them about the stock market. Colonel Blood invested money for the sisters, using the advice provided to them by Vanderbilt, and they soon found themselves wealthy.

Now a financially secure Victoria Woodhull could turn her attention to the fight for women's rights. The American women's rights movement had formally begun in Seneca Falls, New York in 1848 when a small group of women embarked on the long struggle for equal rights. Elizabeth Cady Stanton and Lucretia Mott organized the

Seneca Falls convention and suffered fierce protests from
the movement's opponents who jeeringly called it "The
Reign of the Petticoats."

Even in the face of this hostility the reformers perse-
vered and the movement grew over the years. Still,
despite the fact that more than twenty years had passed
since the movement's beginning, it was in many ways in
its infancy when Victoria became involved. The majority
of women still were not demanding equal rights. Many
women, such as the powerful Catharine Beecher and
Harriet Beecher Stowe—the author of *Uncle Tom's
Cabin*—actually opposed women's rights. They argued
that a woman's proper role was to support their fathers,
brothers, and husbands in their active roles in life.

The Beecher family was highly influential. The sisters
spoke out against women's suffrage (allowing women to
vote.) They were highly articulate and able to sway public
opinion by the power of their oratory and writings. Their
brother Henry Ward Beecher was probably the most
famous and influential preacher of the era. The family
was from Boston and believed deeply in the superiority
of the wealthy, educated class over the poorer masses.
These attitudes, particularly on the part of the sisters, were
certain to create conflicts with an upstart women's rights
advocate like Victoria Woodhull.

Victoria's first real foray into women's rights took
place in January of 1869. One wintry afternoon she
traveled by train from New York to Washington, D.C. to

Commodore Cornelius Vanderbilt was the wealthiest man in America when he helped Victoria and Tennessee establish their stock brokerage firm.

attend the first National Female Suffrage Convention ever held in the nation's capital. Women's rights activists came from all over the country to attend the convention. Victoria soon discovered that the movement was divided, however. She wasted little time before becoming involved in the conflict.

During the Civil War most women leaders had been united over the goal of ending slavery and had worked together. In the war's aftermath, however, the movement split over issues that had been fermenting since 1860. Chief among these was the issue of divorce. The radicals, led by Susan B. Anthony and Elizabeth Cady Stanton, supported divorce. The moderates, including the Beecher sisters, did not.

Though Victoria did not formally participate in the convention that year, she observed the proceedings. She was particularly attuned to Elizabeth Cady Stanton, a well-educated New Englander. Though Victoria admired Stanton's approach to women's rights, she was also critical of Stanton's elitism. Like most of the women involved in the suffrage movement, Stanton came from a privileged background. Victoria realized that a woman from a modest background, without family connections or education, had little chance of making an impact among this group. The women's rights movement was elitist like many other aspects of American life.

After the conference Victoria returned to New York determined to find a way to distinguish herself among the

Harriet Beecher Stowe developed a deep hatred of Victoria.

women reformers. She gave up her professional life as a clairvoyant. She needed all of her energies to prepare for her new role in the movement.

Her first task was to determine what her role was to be. Her answer to this question was unique. Victoria decided to become the first woman on Wall Street, a position she knew would capture the country's attention.

By September 24, 1869, Victoria was on her way to realizing her goal. September 24 was Black Friday on Wall Street. The market crashed when investment banker Jay Gould attempted to corner the gold market, and failed. Investors panicked and began to sell their stock. Victoria sat outside the exchange that day and bought up bargains from the desperate traders on tips provided by Commodore Vanderbilt. By the end of 1869 Victoria had $700,000 in her account.

Confident that they could become powerful players on Wall Street, Victoria and Tennessee approached Commodore Vanderbilt with an offer. They wanted an office on Wall Street and needed his backing to make their financial firm a successful reality. To sway his decision Victoria told the Commodore that her spirit guides had told her to become involved in the exclusively male financial arena. The Commodore responded positively to their proposal and gave the sisters a $7,000 check as a sign of his continued support.

Armed with the Commodore's backing, Victoria and Tennessee became the first female stockbrokers on Wall

A contemporary newspaper illustration of the offices of Woodhull, Claflin & Company.

Street. They named their firm Woodhull, Claflin & Company, and they put a picture of the Commodore up on the wall of their offices. In this new role of businesswoman, Victoria called herself a "representative woman" because she believed that her actions had a value for all women. The poet Walt Whitman paid a visit and confirmed this point with the words, "You have given an object lesson to the whole world....You are a prophecy of the future."

The sisters' entrance on Wall Street generated a great deal of press coverage and eventually the audience Victoria most wanted arrived on the scene. In March of 1870 Susan B. Anthony came to call at the offices of Woodhull, Claflin & Company at 44 Broad Street. Anthony arrived to interview the sisters for the suffrage newspaper, *Revolution*. On the day of the interview, however, Anthony spoke with Tennessee and not Victoria, who sometimes experienced fits of nervousness before important events.

During the interview Tennessee stretched the truth about her and Victoria's background. She claimed to be descended from the wealthy Scottish retailer who shared the last name of Claflin. The exuberant Tennessee also exaggerated her father's past successes. Despite Tennessee's lies Anthony left the office impressed. In her article she wrote: "These two ladies (for they are ladies) are determined to use their brains, energy, and their knowledge of business to earn them a livelihood." Perhaps the greatest praise was Anthony's statement that, "The advent of this woman's firm in Wall Street marks a new era."

Women's suffrage leader Susan B. Anthony interviewed Tennessee Claflin for her newspaper, *Revolution.*

As the first women on Wall Street, Victoria and Tennessee also focused on their public roles. They did not keep traditional business hours only. Sometimes they opened their offices for evening soirees and Sunday afternoon salons. This way they became acquainted with a diverse group of the most powerful and influential men of their time. A typical guest list included such people as William S. Hillyer, President Grant's wartime chief of staff; Jesse Wheelock, the president of the Stock Exchange Board; and Josiah Warren, a prominent American philosopher. Along with businessmen and politicians, reporters from all the major newspapers attended, and gave the sisters plenty of free press.

In their relationships with men Victoria and Tennessee made sure that they maintained the upper hand. Even Colonel Blood became a tool for his ambitious wife. In the brokerage firm contract Victoria did not give her husband ownership. Instead Blood was paid a salary in exchange for his skillful management and professional expertise. Blood did not resent this status, nor was he jealous of Victoria's relationships with powerful men. Whenever Victoria and Tennessee dined with Commodore Vanderbilt, Blood purposefully stayed away. He, like his wife and Tennessee, was well aware that their femininity had a big influence on the success of their transactions with men.

Stephen Pearl Andrews, one of Victoria's most influential male friends at the time, was neither a businessman

Stephen Pearl Andrews helped to ease Victoria's entry into national politics.

nor a traditional politician. A radical reformer and pioneering sociologist, Andrews was also a lawyer and had a medical degree. He spoke thirty languages, including Chinese, and was working to develop a universal language called "Alwato." Andrews believed in feminism and supported his wife Esther's decision to study medicine. He had been involved in all the major issues of the day. When he met Victoria he was sixty-one-years-old with a wealth of experience behind him. Thirty-one-year-old Victoria understood that this man was the perfect person to help her establish herself as a representative woman of her time. She asked him for help.

With Andrews as a friend and teacher, Victoria polished her basic reading and writing skills and began to develop intellectual self-confidence. More than anyone else, Andrews helped Victoria prepare herself for her next challenge—running for the presidency of the United States.

# Chapter Four

## Politics

On April 2, 1870, the *New York Herald* began to publish a series of articles by Victoria Woodhull. The very first article was a bombshell. Victoria declared herself a candidate for the highest office in the land:

> While others of my sex devoted themselves to a crusade against the laws that shackle the women of the country, I asserted my individual independence; while others prayed for the good time coming, I worked for it; while others argued the equality of woman with man, I proved it by successfully engaging in business; while others sought to show that there was no valid reason why women should be treated, socially and politically, as being inferior to man, I boldly entered the arena of politics and business and exercised the rights I already possessed. I therefore claim the right to speak for the unenfranchised women of the country, and announce myself as a candidate for the Presidency.

In 1870, Ulysses S. Grant, a Republican and Civil War hero, was in his first term as president of the United States. Most people assumed that he would run for a second term in 1872. The Democrats had not yet chosen a candidate, but it certainly wouldn't be a woman. If Victoria wanted to run she had to nominate herself and then marshal enough support to get her name on the ballot. As she set about doing this, she remembered the words of the young man in the vision who told her she would one day be "a great leader." Victoria had the utmost self-confidence and faith in herself.

Following her announcement, Victoria leased a house between Madison and Fifth Avenues in New York's Murray Hill district, one of the city's wealthiest and most aristocratic neighborhoods. The mansion was a brownstone that stood four stories high. Inside, chandeliers illuminated frescoed ceilings and ornately decorated marble-lined walls. Victoria kept birds in the greenhouse and at the top of the staircase she placed a painting depicting the loves of Venus. The house was part of a grand statement she was making about herself. To complete the process Victoria bought a newspaper that she called *Woodhull & Claflin's Weekly*.

During this era owning a newspaper gave someone great power. Victoria's paper provided her with a tool for reaching and influencing the public. The first issue of the *Weekly* came out on May 14, 1870. Printed on the highest-quality paper and sixteen pages in length, the paper

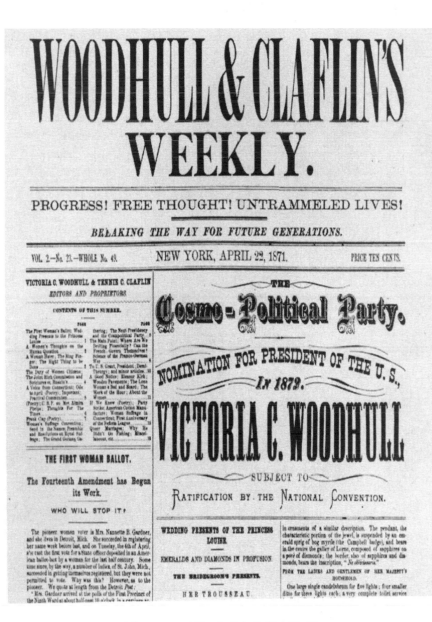

A front page of *Woodhull & Claflin's Weekly*.

looked like a first-class journal. This premiere issue featured a story by the controversial French writer, George Sand, who was known for her emancipated views and her unconventional and somewhat scandalizing style of dressing in men's clothes. The newspaper's statement of purpose announced that:

> This journal will be primarily devoted to the interests of the people and will treat all matters freely and without reservation. It will support Victoria C. Woodhull for President, with its whole strength; otherwise it will be untrammeled by party or personal considerations, free from all affiliation with political or social creeds, and will advocate Suffrage without distinction of sex!

The paper's organization reflected the influence of the multi-talented Stephen Pearl Andrews. Unlike other newspapers that specialized in finance or politics or women's issues, Victoria's *Weekly* integrated all three concerns. Bringing together so many issues paved the way for Victoria to appeal to a variety of interest groups. It also made this diverse audience recognize that they had shared concerns. Unlike the majority of women's rights activists, Victoria declared herself a woman interested not only in women's rights issues but also in human rights issues.

Victoria's newspaper quickly found a wide-ranging

audience. By the fall of 1870, the *Weekly* had a circulation of twenty thousand and had won Victoria a reputation in the public arena. That autumn the newspaper began publishing a series devised by Andrews called, "The Origins, Tendencies and Principles of Government." The series expanded on the ideas found in other women's rights newspapers such as the *Revolution* and was read by people interested in other areas of political reform. One critic wrote that the *Weekly* was "a handsome and readable paper." Her newspaper helped to create the image that Victoria coveted. Powerful and intelligent people began to think of her as a learned woman who was qualified to be president. With the circulation of her newspaper, Victoria was re-inventing herself in the public arena.

Victoria did not stop with the *Weekly*. She knew there was much more to be done if she wanted to establish herself as a committed activist and reformer. Gaining women the right to vote would be crucial in terms of empowering her candidacy. Victoria decided to make herself felt as a woman with a forceful political voice. She moved into the Willard Hotel in Washington, D.C. and declared herself a lobbyist on behalf of women's suffrage. It was a bold move. Never before had a female activist set up residence in the heart of the male-dominated political battlefield of Washington, D.C. Yet Victoria felt comfortable in the swank, bustling hotel. After all, she liked being at the heart of the action.

Now that she had arrived Victoria needed to find the right person to help her forge the right connections. The person who came to her aid was Benjamin Butler, a Massachusetts congressman and Civil War legend. Just as Vanderbilt had helped Victoria navigate the world of finance and Andrews had helped her in the world of ideas, Benjamin Butler eased her way into the political arena.

Victoria continued to be a bold thinker as she worked as a political lobbyist. While most women's suffrage activists were focused on passing a constitutional amendment, Victoria and Benjamin Butler came to the conclusion that an amendment was not necessary. Their argument was simple—they decided that under current law women already had the right to vote. The Fifteenth Amendment stated that the "right of citizens of the United States to vote shall not be denied or abridged" and the Fourteenth Amendment said that all persons born or naturalized in the United States are citizens. Therefore, all citizens, including women, have the constitutional right to vote. It was a stunningly logical argument and both Victoria and Benjamin Butler believed that it was irrefutable.

Victoria persuaded Butler to grant her the opportunity to be the first woman to address Congress and read their findings out loud. Because of his immense influence in the capital, Butler was able to grant Victoria's request.

On January 11, 1871 Victoria Woodhull became the first woman to address a congressional committee. Standing before the committee in an elegant plum-colored

Victoria became the first woman to address a congressional committee on January 11, 1871.

gown with a white rose at her throat, Victoria cut a striking and respectable figure. In her speech she declared that a women's suffrage amendment was unnecessary because women already had the right to vote. Suffrage was the civil right of all citizens. Women were citizens; therefore women had the right to vote.

One of the committee members said Victoria had presented the case "in as good a style as any congressman could have done." The women suffragists attending the committee meeting were also extremely impressed. Afterwards one of them stated that Victoria was "a born queen, and I owe her the allegiance of my heart."

Despite this positive reception, only two members of the committee voted in support of granting women the right to vote. Victoria had succeeded in gaining the recognition of crucial women suffragists, however, including Susan B. Anthony who sent her the following letter: "Dear Woodhull, I have just read your speech of the sixteenth. It is ahead of anything, said or written— bless you dear soul for all you are doing to help strike the chains from woman's spirit."

Victoria's enthusiasm and her enterprising way of getting things done in the nation's capital helped revitalize the women's movement. She became a popular public speaker. This humbly born woman from Ohio was making a name for herself among the blue-blooded leaders of the women's rights movement.

Following her triumphant work in Washington, D.C.,

Victoria was invited to be the keynote speaker at a gathering of the National Woman's Suffrage Association in New York. The gathering was held to ratify the opinions that Victoria had popularized in Washington, D.C. that year: the fact that women already had the right to vote because of the Fourteenth and Fifteenth Amendments to the Constitution.

As the convention progressed Victoria revealed that she had much more in mind than the single issue of women's right to vote. She told the assembly that she was no longer satisfied with the existing Republican and Democratic political parties. In her eyes, the Democrats were tainted by their link to the slave South and the Republicans were unacceptable because of their history of political corruption. "Therefore," she began, "it is my conviction...that it will be equally suicidal for the woman suffragists to attach themselves to either of these parties...."

Victoria went on to read the platform of her new Cosmopolitical Party. Beginning with the demand for suffrage, the traditional battle cry of women's rights, Victoria continued by stating the importance of a political party that defined itself along humanitarian lines. With this strong opening, she addressed the specifics of her radical platform. She wanted a one-term presidency with a lifetime seat in the senate for former presidents, as well as a reform of the U.S. monetary system. She also spoke of national public education and institutionalized welfare for the poor.

Many of these ideas are still controversial today. But the most hotly contested of Victoria's suggestions was a proposal that would prevent the government from passing laws that encroached upon individual freedom. Victoria opposed all laws that interfered with "the right of adult individuals to pursue happiness as they may choose." Her position on individual freedom was in support of those in favor of free love. While the term "free love" seems wildly radical, in reality what the "Free Lovers" wanted was not so extreme. They were opposed to the current marriage laws because they bound a woman unfairly to a man by making her a submissive helpmate to her husband's authority. Both the Free Lovers and Victoria wanted a reform of the marriage laws that would make husband and wife equal partners who entered into the relationship on the basis of love and free will, not obligation and force.

Because her life had made her aware of the contradictions between the roles of men and women, Victoria had grown impatient with what she saw as hypocrisy. Why should Victorian women and men have to pretend to be proper and genteel on the surface when the reality of the situation was far different? Victoria knew that men often had mistresses or went to prostitutes while their wives were expected to remain "Angels of the House." Victoria knew that before women could be equal to men society must change the way it viewed a woman's role in marriage.

This studio portrait of Victoria was taken in 1872.

While a number of people admired Victoria for this open announcement of her views, just as many criticized her. Among Victoria's most dangerous and outspoken critics were Catharine Beecher and Harriet Beecher Stowe. These two sisters strenuously opposed women's suffrage and were heavily critical of Victoria's vocal advocacy in her newspaper and in her speeches. The Beecher sisters also had a score to settle with Victoria because she had aggressively attacked seventy-one-year-old Catharine Beecher in the *Weekly* for her anti-suffrage position.

Ultimately, it was the younger of the two, Harriet Beecher Stowe, who became Victoria's most virulent enemy. Harriet seemed to truly hate Victoria, although the two women had a great deal in common. Like Victoria, Harriet had endured an extremely unhappy marriage. Her husband's disrespectful treatment of her made Harriet ill. She stayed away from her home for more than a year and only returned after her husband promised to treat her more justly. Given Harriet's experience, it would have been understandable if she had supported Victoria's position. Instead, Harriet referred to Victoria as "a snake who should be given a good swat with a shovel."

To "swat" Victoria, Harriet invented a newspaper serial entitled "My Wife and I" that began appearing in the *Christian Union*. The serial introduced a lusty, badly spoken political candidate and newspaper writer named Audacia Dangyereyes who readers immediately identified as a satirical portrait of Victoria Woodhull. Audacia

Victoria knew a scandalous secret about Henry Ward Beecher, America's most famous minister.

smoked, drank, flirted outrageously with men, and edited a newspaper based on the wildest principles of modern French communism and that attacked Christianity, the family, and marriage. In other words, it was a scathing portrait that reached the *Christian Union's* 133,000 subscribers every week.

Harriet Beecher Stowe wanted nothing less than the total destruction of Victoria's credibility. She was horrified by Victoria's political views. But her hatred of Victoria also had a more personal foundation. Harriet Beecher Stowe knew that Victoria possessed damaging information about Harriet's famous brother, Reverend Henry Ward Beecher, who was the first pastor of the exclusive Plymouth Church in Brooklyn, New York. Reverend Beecher was a sensual man with a very high opinion of himself and a renowned position in religious circles. Victoria had learned of an affair that Beecher was having with Elizabeth Tilton, who was the wife of one of Beecher's young colleagues named Theodore Tilton. Not only had Victoria learned of the affair, she knew that Elizabeth Tilton had miscarried a child that her husband believed was Beecher's. In order to prevent Victoria from damaging her brother's reputation, Harriet Beecher Stowe was determined to destroy Victoria's first.

Harriet's attacks intensified and Victoria began to cast around for a prominent person to champion her own point of view. That person arrived in May of 1871 when

Theodore Tilton appeared on Victoria's doorstep. A gifted writer, Tilton was the perfect person to champion Victoria and combat Harriet Beecher Stowe's negative portrait.

Tilton was thirty-five when he stepped into Victoria's life. Handsome as "a perfect Adonis," Victoria and Tilton soon became friends and perhaps even lovers. Victoria asked Tilton to write her biography. She told him embellished stories of her childhood and early womanhood. Theodore enthusiastically undertook the writing and proclaimed, "I shall swiftly sketch the life of Victoria Claflin Woodhull: a young woman whose career has been as singular as any heroine's in a romance."

The biography was published in September of 1871 and sold for ten cents a copy. Victoria was entirely pleased with the resulting book and said it "sparkled in every line like rare old wine."

# Chapter Five

## Scandal

During the 1870s, workers around the world began to protest against poor living and working conditions. In March of 1871, the Commune of Paris reestablished itself in opposition to the government of the Third Republic in France. The Commune was allied with Karl Marx's International Workingmen's Association (IWA) that was founded seven years earlier. By 1871 the IWA had branches in the major cities of Europe and the United States. The IWA wanted to empower the working man during the early years of the Industrial Revolution.

The growth of the IWA in the United States reflected the working man's change in status after the middle of the nineteenth century. Most U.S. workers were no longer independent tradesmen who took pride in their work and had the strong sense of vocation and individual identity that comes from working at a skilled trade. They worked in large, anonymous factories for hourly wages. The workday was twelve to sixteen hours and with the swell of immigrants into U.S. cities people competed heavily for jobs. Factory owners essentially controlled the lives of their employees. The American branches of the IWA tried to give some of the power back to the workers. By 1871, the IWA counted 300,000 American members and was still growing.

In July of 1871 Victoria joined the IWA and she and Tennessee were named heads of the IWA's Section 12 in New York City. Victoria's decision to join the IWA was motivated both by humanitarian reasons and by self-interest. She sincerely empathized with the plight of American workers, but she also understood that labor would provide her with a powerful constituency in her run for the presidency. Victoria was broadening the initial appeal she established among women's rights activists and through her newspaper.

Section 12 soon became the leading American branch of the IWA, in part because Victoria's *Weekly* ran articles supporting its positions, including a declaration of support for the controversial Paris Commune. In August the paper printed an interview with Karl Marx, the founder of the communist movement. Victoria was consciously making herself a friend of the working man and of labor reform.

In July of 1871 she was nominated as a presidential candidate of the Equal Rights Party, a party with a philosophy of labor reform open to both men and women. In her acceptance speech Victoria hearkened back to the initial power her mother recognized in her name:

"Victoria." "I have sometimes thought," she told her audience, "that here is something providential and prophetic in the fact that my parents conferred upon me a name which forbids the very thought of failure."

After the nomination Victoria continued to broaden her alliances. She also formed a closer alliance with America's Spiritualists. The Spiritualists tended to be liberal. They supported feminism and many even believed in communism, which was particularly controversial. The Spiritualists were drawn to reform movements because they saw reform as a way to attain higher human development and personal fulfillment. Furthermore, the Spiritualists were ideal supporters for a woman who wanted to be president of the United States because they believed that women made the best mediums. They placed women in positions of authority and respect within their own organization.

Victoria thought that the Spiritualists represented a potentially larger constituency than either the suffragists or the labor reformers. If she could harness their support she would gain a great deal of power. In his biography of Victoria, Theodore Tilton worked to further her appeal with this group. Tilton stressed Victoria's reliance on spirits in going about her daily life. He went so far as to write that, "She has entertained angels, and not unawares. These gracious guests have been her constant companions. They dictate her life with daily revelations; and like St. Paul, she is not disobedient to the 'heavenly vision.'"

Victoria was well received by the Spiritualists. In

Theodore Tilton wrote a glowing biography of Victoria.

September of 1871, she lectured in Vineland, New Jersey. Later that fall she spoke at their national convention in Troy, New York, with great success.

Initially, women's rights activists were tolerant of Victoria's decision to establish a wider net of support through alliances with such groups as the IWA and the spiritualists. However, in the near future this strategy would create conflict in her relationship with feminist leaders.

Throughout the summer and fall of 1871 Victoria lectured across the United States. Traveling by train, she visited Philadelphia, Pittsburgh, Detroit, Cleveland, Chicago, and Buffalo to speak on the woman's right to vote. Then, on November 3, 1871, together with Tennessee, Victoria registered to vote at the polls in New York City. When the polls opened four days later for the local elections, Victoria and a number of other women headed for the polling booths ready to test their right to vote as United States citizens. When Victoria tried to give her ballot to the presiding official, however, he refused to accept it.

"By what right," she asked, "do you refuse to accept the vote of a citizen of the United States?"

"By this," said the man, showing her a copy of the first constitution of the State of New York.

The first constitution declared that all males and not all citizens have the right to vote. Victoria and the other women were turned away. The attempt at voting had been unsuccessful.

A newspaper rendition of Victoria's nomination for president by the Equal Rights Party.

Despite this setback, Victoria was not discouraged. Although she was committed to a woman's right to vote, she also believed that there were larger issues at stake. Chief among Victoria's concerns was the issue of a woman's rights in marriage. As the fifteen-year-old wife of Canning Woodhull, Victoria had learned what is was like to be considered the legal property of a destitute husband. She was committed to getting women the right to end a bad marriage and to begin anew without being stigmatized by society.

At the time a divorced woman risked losing everything. Society considered a divorced woman an immoral outcast. She could also lose her children, who were considered the property of their father. Such circumstances left women few choices. Either they remained in bad marriages, or they ran the risk of losing their reputations and their children, and found themselves forced to eke out a life for themselves on the margins of society.

It was these concerns that Victoria began speaking about on the lecture circuit. She entitled one speech: "The Principles of Social Freedom, Involving the Question of Free Love, Marriage, Divorce, and Prostitution." Victoria did not equate a woman's right to divorce her husband with free love in a literal sense. But the press and a large percentage of the public often willfully misinterpreted her message.

On the evening of November 20, 1871, Victoria delivered the controversial speech at Steinway Hall in New York. Addressing an audience packed into every seat on

Victoria was turned away when she tried to vote in 1871.

the ground floor and the standing in the aisles, Victoria was introduced by Theodore Tilton. To defend her position that men should not be allowed to continue an oppressive rule over women, Victoria passionately spoke of her own experiences and knowledge:

I have a better right to speak, as one having authority in this matter, than most of you have, since it has been my province to study [the marriage bond] in all its various lights and shades. When I practiced clairvoyance, hundreds, aye, thousands of desolate, heart broken men as well as women, came to me for advice. And they were from all walks of life, from the humblest daily laborer to the haughtiest dame of wealth. The tales of horror, of wrongs inflicted and endured, which were poured into my ears, first awakened me to a realization of the hollowness and rottenness of society, and compelled me to consider whether the laws which were prolific of so much crime and misery as I found to exist should be continued....I know I speak the truth...when I say that thousands of the most noble, loving natured women by whom the world has ever blessed, prepared for, and desirous of pouring their whole life into the bond of union...have all had these generous and warm impulses thrust back upon them by the rude monster into which the previous gentleman has developed.

This cartoon by Thomas Nast cleverly summarized public opinion about Victoria.

When someone in the audience called out, "Are you a free lover?" Victoria did not hesitate. "Yes!" she said in her most elegant voice. "Yes. I AM A FREE LOVER!" In the hush that swept over the astonished audience, Victoria said, "I have an inalienable, constitutional, and natural right to love whom I may, to love as long or as short a period as I can, to change that love every day if I please! And with that right neither you nor any law you can frame have any right to interfere."

In full, Victoria's speech lasted two hours. But she was unable to win the audience over to her side. Instead of focusing on the rational side of her speech—her belief that women should not become social outcasts should they choose divorce—most people left with the idea that Victoria Woodhull was a scandalous Free Lover.

Most newspapers ignored the argument at the core of her speech and concentrated instead on the passionate outburst about free love. The reviews were scathing. The *New York Herald* called the speech "the most astonishing doctrine ever listened to by an audience of Americans," and condemned those who not only applauded but also those who stayed and listened to Victoria's message. The *Independent* said that she spoke "with a mouthful of dirt."

Victoria was not only criticized for the content of her speech but also for her language. She used such words as pregnancy and abortion that were taboo at the time. The most persistent and damaging coverage was on her use of the expression "free love." She again tried to explain what she meant. "What I asked for was educated love that one's daughter be taught to love rightly." The damage was done, however, and Victoria's clarification fell upon dead ears.

The scandal did increase the public's interest in her. Invitations to speak at other locations began to pour in. Yet it was the scandalous Victoria Woodhull whom people primarily wanted to hear, and not the visionary social reformer.

Victoria's reputation was hurt again when, in April 1872, Dr. Canning Woodhull died. The unsavory details of his alcoholism made front-page news. One newspaper reporter wrote that the doctor had been "much addicted to the use of opium and liquor." This sordid information about Victoria's first husband only added to her image as a wild free lover and advocate of communism. The public also learned that Victoria had continued to take care of the debilitated Canning Woodhull after her divorce. Though there was nothing romantic about this relationship, which Victoria viewed strictly as her duty to the father of her children, her enemies accused her of bigamy. They completely ignored the fact that she was acting as a Victorian woman was supposed to act—with mercy.

Victoria maintained a proud exterior. She still planned to be considered as a serious candidate for the upcoming presidential elections. She was determined to rise above public criticism. Unfortunately, Victoria failed to understand the intentions of important women's rights leaders, including Susan B. Anthony. This conflict would sink Victoria's chances to become the first woman president.

Victoria wanted to use the upcoming meeting of the National Woman's Suffrage Association as a forum to elaborate on her own concerns about labor and social issues. She did not want to focus only on women's rights. In the *Weekly* she advertised the meeting as "a grand consolidated convention" of all reformers and not just suffragists. By advertising the meeting in this way Victoria succeeded in attracting a number of reformers from many walks of life. There were the financial reformers, Angela Tilton and her husband, Ezra H. Heywood; a diverse group of spiritualist leaders that included the educator Belva Lockwood; as well as iconoclast John Murray Spear, the founder of an utopian community.

Unlike suffragist leaders Elizabeth Cady Stanton and Susan B. Anthony, many of the reformers who heeded Victoria's call to come to the national meeting came from the lower classes. Like Victoria, they had risen to prominence through their natural talents, hard work, and courage. They were strong supporters of Victoria's run for the presidency.

Victoria's decision to broaden the purpose of the meeting conflicted with the intentions of members of the women's rights movement. They did not want the issue of woman's suffrage diverted by other concerns. When Victoria tried to draw the attendees into a discussion of

Victoria thought that Elizabeth Cady Stanton would support her effort to widen participation in the female suffrage movement.

broader topics of human rights, she lost the support of Susan B. Anthony and other leaders whose backing she had initially coveted.

As a result, after the meeting of May 9, 1872, Victoria found herself at the head of a new group of women activists who were more radical and wide-ranging in their focus than the radical wing of the women's movement.

On May 10, these reformers met to nominate a presidential and a vice presidential candidate on the Equal Rights Party ticket. Victoria delivered an address entitled "Political, Social, Industrial, and Educational Equity," in which she spoke of her dream of equality of all people:

> I would have every workingman or working woman feel that he or she is the equal in all respects to any wealthy person....When this movement overturns the old systems, the millions now paid into the pockets of Wealth will remain in the pockets of industrial people, and instead of there being the very rich few, and the very poor many, all will be rich enough to have all the comforts that wealth and enjoyment demand.

After delivering this energetic, idealistic speech, Victoria was nominated as the presidential candidate of the Equal Rights Party. The nomination was received with cheers and applause. Frederick Douglass, the fa-

mous African American leader of the anti-slavery movement was chosen as the vice presidential candidate.
Following the nomination, the audience sang:

> Yes! Victoria we've selected
> For our chosen head:
> With Fred Douglass on the ticket
> We will raise the dead.

A writer for the *Sun* reported on the exuberant proceedings: "Women waved their handkerchiefs and wept, men
shouted themselves hoarse and perfect confusion pre-
vailed."

# Chapter Six

## Disaster

One month after her May 10, 1872, nomination by the Equal Rights Party, Victoria's fortunes changed for the worse. She had spent thousands of dollars on fund-raising and given $100,000 to the cause of women's suffrage. Now her savings were depleted and by publicly allying herself with workers she had alienated herself from key supporters such as Commodore Vanderbilt and the businessmen she knew from Wall Street. The brokerage business lost its clients. She was soon broke. In recalling this period later Victoria wrote: "Those with whom we had transacted business were sought out, their minds poisoned against us. To our astonishment one by one they fell away until we stood alone. . .completely ruined financially."

There were other problems in the future. America was heading towards the worst recession of the century. Railroad construction had been growing at a rate of twelve percent each year. This overbuilding eventually created a glut. When the railways stopped building some

4,000 businesses collapsed in 1872 alone. By September of 1873 most American railroads were bankrupt and by 1876 over 18,000 businesses had failed. Unemployment skyrocketed until it seemed to overwhelm the country with bands of idle workers.

As Victoria's wealth dwindled away so did her supporters. She had already alienated Susan B. Anthony, and now other women suffragists began to desert her. Even Theodore Tilton, her onetime friend and biographer, campaigned for a different presidential candidate, Horace Greeley, who was running for the Liberal Republican Party. The Equal Rights Party swiftly disintegrated. It was soon apparent to Victoria that she had no chance of winning the presidency.

For a while, conditions only continued to deteriorate. In June of 1872 Victoria was turned out of her house on Twenty-sixth Street. Her landlord said she was too notorious for the quiet, refined neighborhood. Victoria found it difficult to find another place to live. Landlords and hotel managers throughout the city claimed that they were too respectable to have the scandalous Victoria Woodhull in residence.

On June 22, 1872, the *Weekly* had to suspend publication. In August Victoria had to appear in court to be sued for nonpayment of her debts. In court she said that she did not even own the clothes on her back. Publicly humiliated and running out of resources, Victoria finally turned to Henry Ward Beecher for help. She turned to him because he'd once admitted to her—in private conversation—that he shared her views on divorce and free love. Beecher also told Victoria that he would never admit these beliefs publicly. "My dear Victoria," he said, "you are a dangerous radical. Do you realize what happens to militants like you? They are hanged."

Given Beecher's ominous warning, Victoria should have known better than to turn to him, but she did. "My Dear Sir," she began. "My business, my projects, in fact everything for which I live, suffer from [this persecution], and it must cease. Will you lend me your aid in this?" Despite Victoria's plea, Beecher did not help her. Victoria waited in vain for his aid.

Infuriated by what she saw as Beecher's hypocrisy and cowardice, Victoria decided to publicly reveal all the scandalous things she knew about the Plymouth Church's esteemed minister. Victoria felt publicly wronged. In her anger she came to see Beecher's hypocrisy as representative of the hypocrisy prevalent throughout the country. While she was condemned for openly voicing her support for a woman's right to end a miserable marriage, a man like Henry Ward Beecher increased his public authority concealing his views—and his scandalous actions. It irked her even more that he was the brother of the woman who had been calling Victoria a threat to decent people everywhere. If Beecher refused to help her she would expose him as an adulterer and discredit him in the eyes of his supporters, just as she had been discredited.

African-American leader Frederick Douglass was Victoria's vice presidential running mate.

In October of 1872, Victoria revived the *Weekly* in order to publish in graphic detail what she knew about Henry Ward Beecher's adulterous affair. She began the article by stating that she felt no animosity towards Beecher. What outraged her, she said, was his moral hypocrisy:

> I condemn him because I know, and have had every opportunity to know, that he entertains on conviction, substantially the same views I entertain on the social question; that under the influence of these convictions he has lived for many years...in a manner which the religious and moralistic public...condemn; to profess to believe otherwise than as he does believe, to help, persistently to maintain, for these many years that very social slavery under which he was chafing...[makes him] a hypocrite.
>
> The fault with which I therefore, charge him, is not infidelity to the old ideas but unfaithfulness to the new....Speaking from my feelings, I am prone to denounce him as a poltroon, a coward and a sneak.

The 100,000 first printing of the *Weekly* sold out right away when it appeared in newsstands on October 28, 1872. It was so popular that the price for a secondhand copy soared from ten to fifty cents to as much as forty dollars. Everyone wanted "that paper with the Beecher scandal."

Victoria hoped to reap both a financial and a personal reward from the publication. But on November 1, just three days after the *Weekly* hit the newsstands, a Federal warrant for Victoria's arrest was issued. The man behind the charges was Anthony Comstock, a retired merchant and self-appointed moral police force. Comstock arranged to have the *Weekly* charged with obscenity.

After Comstock filed charges, the sisters were arrested and forced to spend four weeks in jail. On Election Day Victoria was in a jail cell when voters wrote her name down as their choice for the United States presidency. It wasn't until the beginning of December that the two sisters were released on $16,000. Two sympathetic supporters came up with the bail money.

After her release, Victoria became even more determined to make Henry Ward Beecher's crimes and hypocrisies known to the public. It seemed doubly unjust that she should be so persecuted while Beecher remained untouched. She began a lecture tour entitled "Moral Cowardice and Modern Hypocrisy," in which she also expressed her outrage at the way she had been persecuted for voicing her views in print. She even appeared in Boston, the Beecher family stomping ground, though she was prohibited from making her speech in the city itself.

Eventually, Victoria had eight rounds of obscenity charges brought against her by Comstock. Time and time again, she was released from jail only to be re-arrested on slightly different versions of the same charge. Given this outrageous treatment, the newspapers picked up on the situation and denounced the U.S. government for censoring Victoria and having her arrested in order to stop the printing of the *Weekly*.

When the obscenity charge trial finally came to court in June of 1873, the judge found Victoria and Tennessee not guilty. Comstock was forced to retreat. Yet they could not rest on this victory for long.

Soon, another man, Luther Challis, brought libel charges against them. In the November 2 issue of the *Weekly*, Tennessee accused Luther Challis, a Wall Street trader, with seducing two young women and then boasting about it in public. Though the sisters were again found not guilty in the trial of March 1874, the continual stress of public harassment and court battles wore Victoria down. For much of this period, she suffered from poor health and depression. She found it difficult to understand how drastically her life had altered in such a short time.

In just two years, Victoria had watched her fortunes rise and fall. The woman who had successfully made it on Wall Street was now broke. Not only was her money gone, she had lost her political authority. Important women's rights leaders such as Susan B. Anthony had deserted her, and her attempts to bring down Henry Ward Beecher had failed. Although Beecher was finally brought to trial by Theodore Tilton the preacher was never publicly humiliated the way Victoria had been. She may have been free of the obscenity and libel charges, but Victoria Woodhull still had a long way to go to restore her fortunes. She was disillusioned with America and felt betrayed.

By the summer of 1873 Victoria was no longer invited to women's conventions. Not only had the women's rights movement abandoned her, but she lost her supporters in labor as well. The humiliation and scandal she endured through the obscenity and libel charges—and her vocal self-defense—isolated her from both of these movements.

Only the Spiritualists continued to stand behind Victoria, but even their support became strained. By September, a large number of Spiritualists split from the national organization because they disagreed with Victoria Woodhull's views. A number objected to her radical beliefs about marriage; others did not believe her to be radical enough. One of the most painful (although true) criticisms came from Judge Edmund S. Holbrooke. He criticized Victoria for using her presidency of the Spiritualist Association as a way to further her aspirations towards becoming president of the United States. Eventually, the association became so divided that they lost their solidarity and broke into a number of petty, warring groups.

Given this constant strain and the instability of living in a series of hotel rooms, Victoria's health worsened.

Then on September 18, 1873, the New York financial world plunged into the worst economic crisis of the century.

The financial crisis hurt Victoria terribly. Already in trouble before the September collapse, afterwards Victoria's economic situation was impossible. Not only was she broke, she was in debt because of the high legal fees she had run up defending herself from the obscenity and libel charges. Her life again resembled the instability of her childhood years. Along with Tennessee and Colonel Blood, Victoria traveled from town to town making political speeches and squeezing out a subsistence existence. During these performances, everyone in Victoria's family participated. Tennie would often read poetry, as would Zula Maud, though Victoria was always the main attraction.

During these months of traveling Victoria's speeches became even more fiery and controversial in their content. The woman who had once acknowledged only a tentative link to the Free Love Movement now declared herself to be "a very promiscuous free lover."

During one speech, Victoria announced: "I want the love of you all, promiscuously. It makes no difference who or what you are, old or young, black or white, pagan, Jew, or Christian, I want to love you all, and be loved by you all, and I mean to have your love."

Scandalous as Victoria's words may initially appear, in reality Victoria was trying to reclaim the support that had once come so easily to her. Deserted by the women's rights, labor, and spiritualism movements she had so energetically supported, Victoria's only recourse was to turn to the ordinary man and woman.

Victoria may have called herself a "promiscuous free lover," but when she caught her husband Colonel Blood with another woman in September of 1876 she filed for divorce on the grounds of adultery. The divorce was granted on October 8 and the marriage and partnership of these two free thinkers came to an end.

Victoria's divorce from James Blood marked a major turning point in her life. After 1876 she began to rethink her beliefs, both private and public. The first woman to run for the United States presidency, the highest office in the land, began to reconsider her very relationship to the country in which she had been born.

# Chapter Seven

## A New Country

Commodore Cornelius Vanderbilt died on January 4, 1877. Vanderbilt was the richest man in America and the richest self-made man in the world. The worth of his holdings was estimated at $100 million. The Commodore's children began to feud over their inheritance after the will was read on January 8. Each of Vanderbilt's eight daughters received $300,000 and his delinquent son, Cornelius Jeremiah, received $200,000. The remainder of the estate went to Vanderbilt's other son William and to William's children. William's siblings felt they had been cheated and decided to take their case to court. They argued that their father was not in his right mind when he wrote his will.

In preparing his defense William became concerned that his siblings would call Victoria and Tennessee as witnesses. The two sisters could reveal the Commodore's fascination with spiritualism. This could endanger William's own claim if it made his father seem to be out of touch with reality in his last years. William decided to get Victoria and Tennessee out of the way. He gave the sisters more than $100,000 to be out of the country so they could not be subpoenaed to testify.

Broke and disillusioned, Victoria was delighted by this financial windfall. She and Tennessee happily took the money and left the country. In August of 1877 Victoria, her two children, her sister, and her mother set sail for England in six first-class staterooms. As Victoria looked toward the sea, she began to imagine a new life for herself across the Atlantic Ocean.

Victoria took a home at 45 Warwick Road in South Kensington, near London. The house was large enough to accommodate her entire family. Many of the scandal ous stories about Victoria followed her overseas. Victoria was feeling more confident and decided to wage a determined campaign to reinvent her history. She began to go by the name of Victoria Woodhall, hoping that this slight change would ally herself with the old, respected Woodhall family in the West of England. She also began publishing a series of "Life Sketches" about herself, in which she borrowed generously from Tilton's flattering biography and added a number of positive comments made about her by people such as Elizabeth Cady Stanton.

Victoria's reputation also made her a public figure. She decided to turn this to her advantage and began a lecture series on the subject of "The Human Body, the Temple of God." She spoke first in Nottingham, then in Liverpool and Manchester. The English audiences expected a scandalous speech from America's most notorious "free lover." What they got instead was a conservative talk on physical hygiene and religion. Although some were disappointed, most found the lecture informative. Most of the newspaper reviews of Victoria's lectures were favorable. A journalist for the *Nottingham Guardian* wrote, "Mrs. Woodhull is unquestionably a great orator, and it is not difficult to understand how she has gained so remarkable a hold upon the people of her own country."

In December Victoria made her London debut. Standing in St. James Hall, Victoria, who was now thirty-nine, wore her chestnut-colored hair loose about her shoulders and a tea rose at her throat. One man in the audience was especially captivated by Victoria. John Biddulph Martin was the co-heir to one of Britain's oldest banks. After seeing and hearing Victoria he resolved to get to know her better. One of Victoria's appeals to John Martin was the fact that her liberal views reminded him of those of his dead sister, Penelope, with whom he had been very close.

Looking back on that first evening, John Martin recalled, "I was charmed with her high intellect, and fascinated by her manner and left the lecture hall that night with the determination that if Mrs. Woodhull would marry me, I would certainly make her my wife."

John Martin's courtship of Victoria progressed very slowly. It was not until September of 1878, some ten months after Victoria's St. James' Lecture, before John

Victoria's daughter, Zula Maud, grew close to her mother after they moved to England.

Martin began to seriously court her. They became formally engaged in December of 1880.

After becoming engaged Victoria began re-inventing her social and political views. Most striking of all was Victoria's passionate denial that she had ever supported the concept of free love. She placed the blame for articles that appeared in the *Weekly* supporting free love on her ex-husband Colonel Blood's shoulders. When Victoria married John Martin on October 31, 1883, almost no trace remained of the vehement free lover who had once denounced marriage as a "hot little hell." Now Victoria worked hard to become what she once denounced—a respectable married woman.

Why did Victoria make such a drastic change? It is possible that she simply did not believe her old convictions anymore. After being hounded by the American public and press for her beliefs on sexual freedom, divorce, and women's rights, it is entirely believable that she could lose faith in some of these ideas. Marrying John Biddulph Martin was a major step away from the tumult of her past. He was a compassionate, intelligent man who loved her enormously. He was also from a highly respected family. She was now a member of the elite class.

Victoria and John moved into an urban mansion at 17 Hyde Park Gate, London. In the coming years, this same section of London was the home of such luminaries as Winston Churchill and Leslie Stephen, the literary father of the modernist writer, Virginia Woolf. Victoria and

Victoria began reinventing her history and her social views after she married J. B. Martin in 1883.

John decorated their home as a retreat from the world. The furnishings were luxurious. There were marble sculptures, purple velvet drapes, and white bearskin rugs on the parquet floors. In the garden, roses perfumed the air, and ivy and jasmine climbed the brick walls. Not only was the house sumptuous and the garden beautiful, but the food prepared there was delicious, too, for they had one of the finest cooks in the city on their household staff.

During this period, Victoria became more and more reclusive. She did make one return to the United States for a lecture tour on "The Scientific Propagation of the Human Race," but the tour was not a success. On her opening night at Carnegie Hall she spoke to a packed house eager for the notorious Victoria's return. But this Victoria was a different person. Now in her fifties, she wore reading glasses as she made her speech on the evolution of man in a quiet, even voice. The evening was not a success, and she and her English husband soon returned to London.

Like her older sister, Tennessee was able to marry a wealthy Englishman. In October 1885, she married Francis Cook, an elderly widower with three grown children. Cook was the head of Britain's largest fabric manufacturer and distributor. As the years passed and their new lives in England took root the famously close sisters began to drift apart.

Although her home was a sanctuary the brick mansion could not protect Victoria from her critics. Victoria's reputation as a free lover followed her to England, and she heard herself labeled an "adventurer" when she married the affluent Martin. During the late 1880s, she received several blackmail threats. Victoria blamed her ex-husband Colonel Blood. In 1886 John Martin hired detectives to find Blood. Only then did Victoria learn that Blood had died of a fever when he went to find gold in Africa in 1885. She now knew that James Blood was not responsible for the threats.

In February of 1894 Victoria, with the help of her devoted husband, began a fight to reclaim her "good name." The British Museum owned six books and pamphlets that cast doubt on Victoria's character. In order to make a public statement about the content of the books Victoria and her husband decided to sue the museum. The case was a last attempt at vindicating herself. With the help of her wealthy husband, she dragged the British Museum through England's court system.

Although it was expensive, Victoria got what she wanted. The court ruled that she was not the scandalous, immoral woman that her press critics accused her of being. The ruling was a symbolic victory for Victoria. She left the courtroom a happy woman who had at last won what she wanted for so long—the restitution of her good name and a chance at respectability.

# Chapter Eight

## Lady Bountiful

In 1895 Victoria returned to publishing. She called her new paper the *Humanitarian*. At first it published articles in the social sciences, but over the years it became more concerned with moral issues. One article, for example, condemned a society that cares more for its pets than its children, citing as evidence that the Society for the Prevention of Cruelty to Animals had a fund of eighty thousand pounds while the Society for the Prevention of Cruelty to Children was broke. The *Humanitarian* also published articles on health, the ongoing activities of the women's movement, and politics. Though the newspaper sold well, the *Humanitarian* lacked the fire that had made *Woodhull & Claflin's Weekly* such a lively journal.

In addition to publishing her newspaper, Victoria began writing her autobiography. She accumulated hundreds of pages on her extraordinary life. She was preoccupied with putting her slant on the issues of her life. In one note to her husband she wrote, "[I am] working hard to undo the wrongs that have been put on me and mine by ignorant bad diseased people...I will not rest until I am known for what I am not what others have made me out to be." Ultimately, Victoria wrote two autobiographies, though she thought neither vindicated her true character. As she continued to write, Victoria reflected, "I wonder whether I shall be able to pen the history of this troubled existence."

As it turned out, she could not. She was never able to write the true story of her life. In March of 1897, her husband John Martin died. He was fifty-five at the time, and he had been completely devoted to his wife. Three days before his death, Martin's eighty-eight-year-old father died. Therefore, when the wills were read Victoria wound up being the inheritor not only of her husband's immense wealth but also of her father-in-law's as well. Victoria inherited the mansion in Hyde Park and a beautiful property called Bredon's Norton, as well as other land in Gloucestershire. At the time of her husband's death Victoria's worth was estimated at 147,129 pounds. She was also the largest shareholder in Martin's Bank.

In 1901, some three year after her husband's death, Victoria sold the *Humanitarian* and left London. She had decided to abandon city life and move to the country house at Bredon's Norton. Many thought that the sixty-eight-year-old Victoria planned to retire, but after her arrival in Bredon's Norton, a village with a declining population and few resources, Victoria and her daughter Zula set about transforming her new home into a "model town." At first she isolated herself from the residents and did not consult them with her plans. She lived high above the village in a Tudor-style mansion of yellow stone.

It was 1906 before Victoria succeeded in getting on proper footing with the villagers. She turned the Manor House at Bredon's Norton into a residential college and club for women. The school opened that fall. Entitled the International Agricultural Club and School of Intensive Petite Culture, it offered a full three-year program as well as short courses. The school was not a success, however. At its peak it enrolled only thirty-one students. In 1911 it was turned into a recreational club for men and women. In addition to the facilities for studying agriculture, there was also golf, boating, croquet, and tennis.

Though the residential college failed, Victoria and her daughter had other plans. In 1907, they opened a model school for children in the village. The curriculum included courses in divinity, history, geography, science, English language and literature, mathematics, and carpentry. There were organized nature walks and health care on site. After the first year, the school began to attract students from surrounding villages. Victoria and Zula hired a bus to bring the children to and from school. Everybody in Bredon's Norton seemed satisfied with the new system of education. But the national government did not find the education up to standards. It was closed in December of 1909. Local children had to be bussed out to a neighboring village to continue their education.

Victoria and Zula standing before their home in Bredon's Norton.

Victoria continued to provide the commuters with a hot meal on school days.

Despite these unsuccessful forays into education Victoria persisted. In the years that followed she became the village's fairy godmother. She organized Christmas pageants with sumptuous banquets and gave out expensive and unusual gifts. She supported youth movements such as a boy's camp that was held on the grounds of her home. She even turned her barn into a local theater.

Victoria enjoyed the new automobiles and could often be seen motoring at high speeds through the countryside. Sitting in the back seat of a chauffeur-driven car, Victoria would call out to her driver to go "faster, faster!"

When World War I erupted in 1914 Victoria plunged into the war effort. She set about making sure that the village had enough supplies on hand to endure the hardships of war. In September of 1914 she began working with the Red Cross. She provided material for local women to make flannel clothes for soldiers and supported the Children's Harvest Home Program. By May of 1915 Victoria was even housing wounded soldiers. She began a campaign to convince the United States to enter the war years before her native country declared war on Germany in 1917.

Victoria's war effort was her final great effort. After the war ended, she withdrew into a quiet life. Although she continued to interact with the villagers at Bredon's Norton she did not socialize much. Tennessee died in

Tennesse drifted away from Victoria after she married Sir Francis Cook.

January 1923, but Victoria was not with her at the time. After Tennessee's marriage to Sir Francis Cook the sisters rarely spoke to each other. Nevertheless, Victoria was pleased to learn that in her final writings Tennessee spoke lovingly of her older sister.

Almost everyone in the area admired Victoria during the closing years of her life. The woman who once stood up in a lecture hall and requested the love of everyone now seemed to have gotten her wish. In the village she was known as "Lady Bountiful" and treated with great respect.

Victoria died in her sleep on June 9, 1927 at the age of eighty-eight. Seven years earlier, in 1920, she had learned that American women had at last been granted the right to vote. Yet her response was not fiery and exuberant. She only professed that she hoped women would use their hard-won right wisely.

At the private funeral service, W.H.B. Yerborough, rector of Bredon's Norton, spoke of Victoria as a woman "in advance of her time." Victoria's children, Zula and Byron, agreed with the reverend's description of their mother. But, although the reverend's pronouncement was undeniably true, it was Elizabeth Cady Stanton who best captured Victoria's tenacious, independent character:

> Victoria Woodhull stands before us today one of
> the ablest speakers & writers of the century:

Victoria and her children in one of her favorite motor cars.

sound & radical, alike in political, religious & social principles. Her face, form, manners & conversation all indicate the triumph of the moral, intellectual, spiritual, over the sensuous in her nature. The processes & localities of her education are little to us, but the grand result is everything.

In the end, Victoria herself would have agreed "the grand result is everything."

# Timeline

1838—Victoria Claflin born in Homer, Ohio, on September 23.
1848—Seneca Falls convention held.
1853—marries Canning Woodhull.
1854—son Byron born.
1855—moves to San Francisco.
1861—daughter Zula Maud born.
1866—marries Colonel James Blood.
1868—moves to New York City.
1869—attends National Female Suffrage Convention.
  —opens Woodhull, Claflin & Company stock brokerage.
1870—starts *Woodhull & Claflin's Weekly*.
1872—runs for president on the Equal Rights Party ticket.
  —arrested for obscenity and slander.
1877—moves to England.
1883—marries John Biddulph Martin.
1895—starts the *Humanitarian* newspaper.
1927—dies on June 9.

# Bibliography

Braude, Ann. *Radical Spirits: Spiritualism and Women's Rights in Nineteenth-Century America.* Boston: Beacon Press, 1989.

Crow, Duncan. *The Victorian Woman.* New York: Oxford Univer sity Press, 1972.

Gabriel, Mary. *Notorious Victoria: The Life of Victoria Woodhull, Uncensored.* Chapel Hill: Algonquin Books, 1998.

Gordon, John Steele. *The Scarlet Woman of Wall Street: Jay Gould, Jim Fisk, Cornelius Vanderbilt, the Erie Railway Wars, and the Birth of Wall Street.* New York: Weidenfeld & Nicholson, 1988.

Matthews, Glenna. *The Rise of Public Woman: Woman's Power and Woman's Place in the United States, 1630-1970.* New York: Oxford University Press, 1992.

Meade, Marion. *Free Woman: The Life and Times of Victoria Woodhull.* New York: Alred A. Knopf, 1976.

Schneir, Miriam, ed. *Feminism: The Essential Historical Writings.* New York: Random House, 1972.

Stanton, Elizabeth Cady, Susan B. Antony et al. *A History of Woman Suffrage.* New York: Arno Press, 1969 (original, 1881).

Stern, Madeleine B. ed. *The Victoria Woodhull Reader.* Weston, Mass.: M&S Press, 1974.

Underhill, Lois Beachy. *The Woman Who Ran for President: The Many Lives of Victoria Woodhull.* New York: Penguin Books, 1995.

# Sources

**CHAPTER ONE**

p.12 "The angels put me..." Underhill, Lois Beachy. *The Woman Who Ran For President*. New York: Penguin Books, 1995, p. 18.

p.13 "One day, you will lead..." Gabriel, Mary. *Notorious Victoria*. Chapel Hill: Alogonquin Press, 1998, p 9.

p.14 "Sinner's, repent!" Meade, Marion. *Free Woman*. New York: Alfred A. Knopf, 1972, p. 1.

p.20 "Be a good listener..." Gabriel, op.cit., p. 11.

**CHAPTER TWO**

p.21 "tell your father..." Underhill, op.cit., p. 23.

p.22 "In a single day..." Meade, op.cit., p. 14.

p.24 "I do not care..." Gabriel, op.cit., p. 16.

p.26 "My dear, send..." Underhill, op.cit., p. 27.

p.26 "Deliver my soul..." Underhill, op.cit., p. 34.

**CHAPTER THREE**

p.33 "One night..." Underhill, op.cit., p. 44.

p.34 "Mrs. Victoria Woodhull..." Underhill, op.cit., p. 44.

p.35 "Do as I do..." Underhill, op.cit., p. 45.

**CHAPTER FOUR**

p.47 "While others..." Underhill, op.cit., pp. 77-78.

p.50 "This journal will..." Gabriel, op.cit., p. 59.

p.51 "a handsome and..." Meade, op.cit., p. 64.

p.54 "in as good a style..." Underhill, op.cit., p. 104.

p.54 "Dear Woodhull..." Gabriel, op.cit., p. 87.
p.55 "Therefore...it is my..." Underhill, op.cit., p. 125.
p.58 "A snake who should..." Meade, op.cit., p. 83.
p.60 "a perfect Adonis" Gabriel, op.cit., p. 114.
p.60 "I shall swiftly sketch..." Gabriel, op.cit., p. 121.
p.61 "sparkled in ever line." Underhill, op.cit., p. 157.

**CHAPTER FIVE**
p.63 "I have sometimes thought..." Gabriel, op.cit., p. 126.
p.64 "She has entertained..." Gabriel, op.cit., pp. 147-148.
p.70 "Are you a free lover?" Meade, op.cit., p. 105.
p.72 "with a mouthful..." Gabriel, op.cit., p. 150.
p.72 "What I asked for..." Gabriel, op.cit., p. 150.
p.76 "I would have..." Underhill, op.cit., pp. 212-213.
p.76 "Yes! Victoria..." Unerhill, op.cit., p. 213.

**CHAPTER SIX**
p.78 "Those with whom..." Underhill, op.cit., p. 214.
p.80 "My dear Victoria..." Gabriel, op.cit., pp. 176-177.
p.80 "My business..." Underhill, op.cit., p. 222.
p.82 "I condemn him..." Underhill, op.cit., p. 222.
p.86 "I want the love..." Gabriel, op.cit., pp. 223-224.

**CHAPTER SEVEN**
p.90 "Mrs. Woodhull is questionably..." Underhill, op.cit., p. 278.
p.90 "I was charmed..." Meade, op.cit., pp. 155-156.

**CHAPTER EIGHT**
p.96 "[I am] working hard..." Meade, op.cit., p. 160.
p.102 "Victoria Woodhull stands..." Stanton, Elizabeth Cady. Letter to Lucretia Mott. Smith College, April 1, 1871.

# Index